Contents

This book is intended as an introduction to the use of census materials in the primary class-room. Census documents can provide children with a fascinating insight into the past and stimulate an awareness of the present. The aim is to present examples of original census material to illustrate the types of information available in the census documents. The book is based on a series of investigations into the past and present for children to work on individually or in groups. It also serves as an introduction to census documents as a valuable teaching resource for teachers who are unfamiliar with them.

The information in the book is based mainly on the 1881 census for Burncross, which was then a small village community about 11 km north of Sheffield. The examples which are used for the investigations in this book are based on the Enumerators' Returns for Districts 7, 8, 9 and 15 in the parish of Ecclesfield, in the county of Yorkshire.

What is a Census?

A census is the official numbering of the inhabitants of a country.

A census is a method of counting all the people who live in a country. In Great Britain the census is taken during one day every ten years.

On that day the names of all the people living in every household in the country have to be recorded on a special census form. The head of the household has to write down the name of every person sleeping in the house on the night of the census. Other information about each person also has to be given.

The first census to be taken by the government in Great Britain was in 1801 and a census has been taken in the first year of every decade ever since. The only exception was 1941, during the Second World War. The most recent census to be taken in this country was in 1981; the next one will be in 1991.

What is the purpose of a census?

The information contained in the census is used for many things. The most important is to tell us how many people there are living in the country. This information is used mainly by the government and local councils when they are planning for the future, such as the building of new schools and hospitals.

In the last census the form contained twenty-one questions. Some of the answers to these questions are private and confidential, so all census information is kept secret for 100 years. The last census to be released was the 1881 census; this can now be used by anyone. It is the 1881 census which provides most of the examples used in this book.

How was the 1881 census organized?

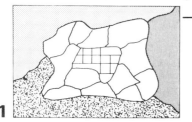

1 Each county in Great Britain is divided up into smaller units. Each unit is called a parish.

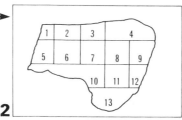

2 For the purpose of the census, each parish is then divided up again into smaller units called Enumeration Districts.

3 A man was appointed to look after each Enumeration District; he was called an Enumerator. He was responsible for organizing the census in that district.

4 The Enumerator delivered a census form to each house in his district.

5 On Sunday, 3 April 1881 the census was taken. The names of all the people sleeping in each house on the Sunday night had to be entered on the census form. It was then possible to count the exact number of people in the country on that day.

6 In 1881 there were many adults who could not read or write. This was because most of them had never been to school. In these cases the census form had to be filled in by the Enumerator.

7 All the information on these census forms was then written out on large sheets of paper by the Enumerator. These were called the Enumerator's Returns. They contained the details of everyone who lived in that district.

8 It is these documents that we can use today to find out about the people who lived in 1881.

ARNOLD-WHEATON

Arnold-Wheaton
A Division of E. J. Arnold & Son Limited
Parkside Lane, Leeds LS11 5TD
and
Hennock Road, Exeter EX2 8RP

A subsidiary of Pergamon Press Ltd
Headington Hill Hall, Oxford OX3 0BW

Pergamon Press Inc.
Maxwell House, Fairview Park, Elmsford, New York 10523

Pergamon Press Canada Ltd
Suite 104, 150 Consumers Road, Willowdale, Ontario M2J 1P9

Pergamon Press (Australia) Pty Ltd
P.O. Box 544, Potts Point, N.S.W. 2011

Pergamon Press GmbH
Hammerweg 6, D-6242 Kronberg, Federal Republic of Germany

First published 1985

Printed in Great Britain by A. Wheaton & Co. Ltd, Hennock Road, Exeter

ISBN 0 560-26535-2

ACKNOWLEDGEMENTS

The statistics in this book are taken from the 1841, 1881 and 1981 censuses; the information is Crown copyright and is reproduced with the permission of the Controller of Her Majesty's Stationery Office.

The table of most popular names in England and Wales in 1875 (p. 8) is drawn from material in *First Names First* by Leslie Dunkling, published by J. M. Dent.

The table of most popular names in 1983 (p. 9) is reproduced by permission of Mrs Margaret Brown and Mr Thomas Brown.

The material on p. 19 is taken from Report of the Children's Employment Commission – Mines, 1842.

The map on pp. 22 and 24 is reproduced from the 1953 Ordnance Survey 1:2500 map with the permission of the Controller of Her Majesty's Stationery Office, Crown copyright reserved.

Photographs are reproduced by permission of The Mansell Collection (p. 15), BBC Hulton Picture Library (p. 19), David Lee (pp. 13, 16), John Monteyne (pp. 21, 22, 23, 24, 25).

Illustrations by Denby Designs and Terry Bambrook

Cover photography: P.J. Photography, St Austell and Studio 4, Exeter

What information can we take from the 1881 census?

Name and surname of each person
The Enumerators' Returns contain the names of all the people living in this country on 3 April 1881. They can be used for a survey of forenames, to discover the most popular names in the 1880s. This column is very useful to anyone trying to discover their own family history: it is possible to trace your ancestors by using census documents.

Age last birthday of males/females
This gives the ages of the people listed in the census. The ages of males and females are listed in two separate columns, males on the left and females on the right. The age is usually given in years only, but in the case of a young baby it is possible to find the words 'months' or 'days' after the number.

Rank, profession, or occupation
This column provides a lot of information about the type of jobs or occupations people had in the 1880s. This information can help us to find out about former local industries of a particular area. The word 'rank' means that if someone had a title such as Lord, Lady or Earl then it had to be entered in this column.

Condition as to marriage
In this column we can find out whether the person was married or unmarried. It will also tell us if the person was a widow or a widower.

NAME and Surname of each Person	RELATION to Head of Family	CON-DITION as to Marriage	AGE last Birthday of		Rank, Profession, or OCCUPATION	WHERE BORN
			Males	Females		
Thomas Hickling	Head	Mar	34		Engin Fitter	Doncaster Yorkshire

Relation to head of family
This column gives the relation of each person to the head of the household. The title 'head' was usually given to the father of the family or to the husband. An unmarried woman with her own house or a woman whose husband had died would be the head of her household.

This information is very useful for a survey on family size because you can easily count the number of people in each family. If anyone else was staying at the house then the words 'lodger', 'visitor' or 'servant' may also appear in the column.

Where born
This column tells us where the people were born. We can see whether they were born in the local area or whether they had moved there from somewhere else. It usually states the village, town or city and the county of birth, though sometimes only the county is given. This information is very useful for anyone tracing their family history.

1981 census results
The most recent census was in 1981, but the information on the Enumerators' Returns must remain secret for 100 years. These will not be released until after the year 2081.

However, the results of the 1981 census are available now in the form of statistics. This means that the answers to all the questions have been collected together and the totals are given in numbers. These results are available for the whole country, for each county and for small areas.

Activities

Do you know what these words mean?
Match the words with the meanings.

1	Widow	A man whose wife has died.
2	Widower	A person renting a room in a house.
3	Cousin	The person in charge of a family.
4	Lodger	A woman whose husband has died.
5	Visitor	Son or daughter of parent's brother or sister.
6	Head	A person staying on a short visit.

Investigating Original 1881 Census Documents

The original census documents are very interesting, especially if you are trying to trace your family history. However, because they were written more than 100 years ago, they are sometimes difficult to read. All the Enumerators' Returns were written by hand, usually in the Victorian 'copperplate' style.

These are a few examples taken from the original 1881 Enumerators' Returns, with some notes to make them easier to understand.

William Cutts	Head	Mar	36		Farm Bailiff	Masham Rotherham Yorks
Ann Cutts	Wife	Mar		36		Rotherham Yorkshire
Elizabeth Cutts	Daughter			13	Scholar	Ecclesfield Do
Thomas H. Do	Son		11		Do	Do Do
Sarah Jane Do	Daut			9	Do	Do Do
Ellen Do	Do			7	Do	Do Do
William Do	Son		5			Do Do

Sometimes the Enumerators used abbreviations when writing out the census return forms. These are some of the common ones:

Daut.
Dau. } Daughter

Serv.–Servant
Widr.–Widower

Gr. Daut.
Gr. Dau. } Granddaughter

'Do' or '-do-' these both mean 'the same as above'

Mar.–Married
Unm.–Unmarried

Charlotte Frear	Head	Widow	38		*	Titchfield Elford
Alfred Edden	Son		13		Scholar	Tamworth Staffordshire
Alice Edden	Daut			9	Do	Ecclesfield Yorkshire
Frank Do	Son		5			Do Do

Joseph Barwood	Head	Mar	60		Farming 20 acers	Ecclesfield Yorkshire
Ann Barwood	Wife	Mar		55		Bradfield Do

Activities

A

1 How many members of the Cutts family were born in Ecclesfield?
2 How many scholars were there in the Cutts family?
3 How many daughters were there in the Cutts family?
4 How many abbreviations can you find on this page?
5 What do you notice about the head of the Frear family?
6 There are two spelling mistakes in the examples on this page. What are they?
7 Find out about the 'copperplate' style of handwriting. Try to write the alphabet in 'copperplate'.

Robert Percivel	Head	Mar	37		Coal Miner	Surfleet Lincolnshire
Clara Percivel	Wife	Do		38		Ecclesfield Yorkshire
William Do	Son		15		Miner	Do Do
Annie Do	Daut			11	Scholar	Do Do
Sarah E. Do	Do			7	Do	Do Do
John W. Donner	Apprentice		16		Coal Miner	Barnsley Do
William Brown	Head	Widower	43		Bricklayer	Sheffield Yorkshire
George L. Brown	Son	Unm	22		Do	Waddington Lincolnshire
John W. Do	Do	Do	20		Miner	Do Do
Mary A. Do	Daut				Maid at Home	Sheffield Yorkshire
Barzillia Do	Daut			16	Do	Do Do
Benjmn. Do	Son		15		Engineer	Do Do
James E. Do	Do			9	Scholar	Do Do
Thomas W. Do	Grandson			2 Months		Ecclesfield Do
George Bolton	Head	Mar	24		Coal Miner	Do Do
Rachel Bolton	Wife	Do		21		Wentworth Do
Ada Do	Daut			4		Chapeltown Do
Thomas Do	Son		2			Do Do
Mary Jackson	Mother	Widow		52		Norfolk
James Allsopp	Head	Mar	35		Miner	Tamworth Staffordshire
Betsy Allsop	Wife	Do		30		Do Do
Joe Do	Son		12		Scholar	Do Do
Peter Do	Do		8		Do	Ecclesfield Yorkshire
Frank Do	Do		2			Do Do
Joe Wilson	Lodger	Unm	32		Coal Miner	Tamworth Staffordshire

This is a copy of a complete page taken from the Enumerators' Returns for the parish of Ecclesfield in 1881. Use the information on this page to answer the following questions. Give your answers in whole sentences.

B

1 How many people were born in Ecclesfield?
2 Who was the oldest person mentioned on the page?
3 Mary A. Brown was a 'Maid at Home'. What do you think this means?
4 How many people were born in Yorkshire?
5 Who was the head of the family with the most children?
6 How old was Thomas Brown?
7 How many different birthplaces are listed?
8 How many girls are listed as being scholars?
9 What is a scholar?
10 Who was a widow and how old was she?
11 Joe Wilson was a lodger with the Allsop family. Where was he born?
12 How many people were miners?
13 John W. Denver was an apprentice: what does this mean?
14 Which girl's name appears twice?
15 What is the name of the youngest married woman?
16 Two children were born in Chapeltown. Who were they?
17 What were the names of William Brown's two eldest sons?

If you are able to obtain some of the 1881 Enumerators' Returns for your own area, have a close look at them. Are any of the occupations listed the same as those mentioned on these pages?

Investigating Forenames

The results of the 1881 forenames survey for the Burncross study area are as follows. The table on the left shows the ten most popular names for the people living in the local area. There were totals of seventy-one different male forenames and seventy different female forenames, taken from the 1881 census.

1881: Burncross study area				
Order of popularity	Males	Number of people	Females	Number of people
1	William	87	Mary	74
2	John	76	Sarah	69
3	George	58	Ann(e)	48
4	Thomas	45	Elizabeth	45
5	Joseph	45	Annie	29
6	James	24	Hannah	22
7	Henry	23	Alice	16
8	Frederick	21	Ellen	15
9	Charles	19	Florence	10
10	Arthur	19	Emily	10

1875: England and Wales		
Order of popularity	Males	Females
1	William	Mary
2	John	Elizabeth
3	George	Sarah
4	Thomas	Annie
5	James	Alice
6	Henry	Florence
7	Charles	Emily
8	Arthur	Edith
9	Frederick	Ellen
10	Joseph	Ada

The table on the right shows the ten most popular names in the whole of England and Wales in 1875. These lists are based on the Registrar General's Indexes of Births.
Compare this list with the list for Burncross in 1881.

Activities

A Draw a block graph to show the top ten male and female forenames in Burncross in 1881. Use the information in the table. (For the vertical axis use 2 cm on the graph paper for every 10 people.)
Colour the male columns in one colour and the female columns in another colour.

B Make a forename survey for your own school

1 Use a set of class lists or registers for your school. Make a tally count of all the different forenames that appear on the lists. (Make *separate* lists for boys' and girls' names.) Set out your lists like those shown in the example.

2 When you have gone through every class, total up all the tally marks for each name.

3 Write out two lists, one for girls and the other for boys, giving the *names* and *totals* in order of popularity.

4 Draw a graph (similar to the one for 1881) to show the top ten boys' and girls' names in your school.

5 Are any of the names in your list the same as those in the 1881 list?

An example of a name tally count	
Peter	///
James	⊬⊬ /
John	/
Alison	⊬⊬ ⊬⊬ /
Julie	////
Clare	//

Another way of carrying out a forename survey is to use a copy of your local newspaper.

Some parents place an announcement in the local newspaper when they have a baby, to tell all their friends. These announcements can usually be found in the 'Births' column, in the classified advertisements.

Some national newspapers, such as *The Times*, also contain these announcements. Every year some people make a survey of the names that appear in this column of *The Times*. These are the results of that survey for 1983.

Boys			Girls		
Order of popularity	Name	No. of times used	Order of popularity	Name	No. of times used
1	James	227	1	Elizabeth	149
2	William	171	2	Louise	106
3	Edward	153	3	Jane	94
4	Alexander	151	4	Mary	81
5	Thomas	145	5	Charlotte	80
6	Charles	123	6	Victoria	75
7	John	122	7	Sarah	74
8	David	105	8	Alice	60
9	Richard	95	9	Katherine	57
10	Robert	92	10	Alexandra	56
				Emily	56

Using your local newspaper, make a survey of the names which appear in the 'Births' column. This survey is best done every day, over a number of weeks or months.

Examples of 'Birth' announcements in newspapers.

C There are twenty-six forenames hidden in this word-square. All the names appear in the 1881 census. There are three mystery names where you are given the first letter as a clue. Find all the names in the word-square and write down the mystery names.

D	A	V	I	D	A	B	E	T	S	Y	C
A	D	A	L	E	L	Y	D	I	A	A	E
N	L	A	L	B	E	R	T	Z	B	B	C
I	S	A	A	C	S	L	P	Q	R	S	D
E	A	J	M	I	U	Q	A	M	A	U	D
L	M	A	Y	E	S	R	U	T	H	R	A
P	U	A	T	L	A	U	L	X	A	A	N
C	E	R	S	L	N	O	G	J	M	A	N
F	L	O	R	E	N	C	E	O	I	L	W
J	A	N	E	N	A	A	M	E	L	I	A
B	N	O	R	A	H	Z	M	L	O	C	R
X	A	G	N	E	S	W	A	L	T	E	R

AARON	EMMA
ABRAHAM	FLORENCE
ADA	ISAAC
AGNES	J . . .
ALBERT	JOEL
ALICE	LYDIA
AMELIA	MAUD
AMY	NORA
ANN	P . . .
BETSY	RUTH
DANIEL	S . . . . .
DAVID	SUSANNAH
ELLEN	WALTER

Make up a 'word-square' of your own, using the names you have collected in the forename survey of your class or school.

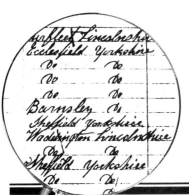

Investigating
Birthplaces

When the 1881 census is used to investigate birthplaces the people living in the area can be divided into three groups. The first group is for the people who were born in the **local area**. The second is for those born in the **same county**, in this case Yorkshire.

It is the third group which is most useful: this is for people who were born in **other parts of the British Isles** or even in **other countries**.

These are the results of the birthplace survey for Burncross.

Total number of people living in Burncross in 1881	3833	
People born in the Burncross area	2315	60%
People born in other parts of Yorkshire	898	24%
People born in other English counties or other countries	620	16%

Birthplaces in other English counties
(The number after each county is the number of people born there.)

1	Derbyshire	92	14	Somerset	11	27	Surrey	3
2	Nottinghamshire	74	15	Cambridgeshire	11	28	Northumberland	3
3	Lincolnshire	63	16	Leicestershire	9	29	Rutland	2
4	Staffordshire	57	17	Suffolk	9	30	Hertfordshire	2
5	Lancashire	39	18	Gloucestershire	8	31	Devonshire	2
6	Norfolk	26	19	Kent	7	32	Buckinghamshire	2
7	Berkshire	26	20	London	7	33	Middlesex	1
8	Oxfordshire	23	21	Worcestershire	6	34	Dorset	1
9	Northamptonshire	22	22	Wiltshire	5	35	Hampshire	1
10	Warwickshire	19	23	Cumberland	5	36	Herefordshire	0
11	Bedfordshire	13	24	Essex	4	37	Sussex	0
12	Shropshire	12	25	Cornwall	4	38	Huntingdonshire	0
13	Durham	12	26	Cheshire	3	39	Westmoreland	0
								584

Birthplaces in other countries

Ireland	18
Wales	10
Scotland	3
America	3
India	1
France	1
	36

This table lists all the other counties in England where Burncross residents were born. Some of the county names are different from those used today: this is because the county boundaries were changed in 1974 and some of the counties were given new names.

Activities

A

1 Copy Map 1 on page 28 and colour in all the counties shown on the list. The numbers in front of each county name match those drawn on the map. Colour the counties according to the number of people born in each county. Choose five different colours and use the key provided.

2 Do the same thing using Map 2 to show how many people were born in the other countries of the British Isles.

3 Using a modern atlas compare the counties of today with those shown on the map for 1881. Which counties are different?

The information has shown that many people who were living in Burncross in 1881 were born in other parts of the British Isles. This movement of people from one place to another is known as **migration**.

In the 1880s families often had to move around the country for the father to find a job. Sometimes the father would go away on his own to look for work and leave his family at home. When he found work he would send them money. Young ladies and teenage girls often went to work away from home, usually as servants in large houses.

In the 1870s and 1880s many men came over from Ireland to work as labourers in the coal-mines or steelworks, or as 'navvies' on the new railways that were being built.

1.Derbyshire 2.Nottinghamshire
3.Lincolnshire 4.Staffordshire

Most of the migration into Burncross was from the counties of Derbyshire, Nottinghamshire, Lincolnshire and Staffordshire. Most of the working men who came from these counties were coal-miners. Many moved into the Burncross area, which was part of the very rich Barnsley coalfield, where jobs were available.

These are some entries from the 1881 Census.

Name:	Relation:	Cond:	Age:	Occupation:	Birthplace:
Sarah Shaw	Servant	Unm.	20	Servant	Hull, Yorkshire
Ruth Butler	Servant	Unm.	18	Servant/Maid	Barrow-in-Furness, Lancashire
William Hicks	Head	Mar.	34	Labourer	Stratford-upon-Avon, Warwickshire
Charles Sylvester	Lodger	Unm.	19	Coal-miner	Tamworth, Staffordshire
Agnes Taylor	Wife	Mar.	32	Servant	Sevenoaks, Kent
Emma Micklethwaite	Wife	Mar.	33	Vicar's Wife	King's Lynn, Norfolk
Samuel Drew	Head	Mar.	60	Doctor	St Austell, Cornwall
Charles Howell	Lodger	Unm.	21	Coal-miner	Worcester, Worcestershire
Daniel Smith	Lodger	Unm.	33	Shoemaker	Spalding, Lincolnshire
Jeremiah Fennesay	Head	Mar.	30	Fireman	Manchester, Lancashire
George Brown	Lodger	Widr	46	Labourer	Ely, Cambridgeshire
Tom Williamson	Head	Mar.	46	Coal-miner	Newcastle, Northumberland
Charles Hodge	Lodger	Unm.	20	Pawnbroker	Liverpool, Lancashire
Ellen Wikeley	Wife	Mar.	47		Southampton, Hampshire
John Pool	Lodger	Unm.	33	Labourer	Birmingham, Warwickshire

B

1 What does 'migration' mean?

2 Who were the people most likely to move in search of work?

3 What was a 'navvy'?

4 Why did many coal-miners come to live in the Burncross area?

C There are fifteen birthplaces given in this list. Their positions have been marked and numbered on Map 3 on page 29.

Using an atlas and the list, identify each birthplace marked on the map and the person who was born there. The birthplaces are *not* numbered in the same order as they appear in the list, so be careful!

When you have identified each birthplace complete the table at the side of Map 3. Using the scale beside the map, work out the approximate distance from each birthplace to Burncross.

Investigating
Family Size

In Victorian times, families were very much larger than they are today. Families with as many as fifteen, or even more, children were quite common. One of the main reasons for this was that as soon as they were old enough to get a job, the children were able to earn extra money to help support the family.

Another reason was that the death rate among young children was very high, so parents had a lot of children to make sure that as many as possible survived. Many children died before they reached one year old, mainly from diseases such as chicken pox, measles, scarlet fever, tuberculosis, and diphtheria. There were no hospitals for the majority of people and no drugs or vaccinations to protect children from these illnesses.

Poor housing and lack of fresh food and pure water also caused many deaths among children, especially in towns and cities. Large families caused problems of overcrowding in small houses. Most of the houes owned by working people would have had two bedrooms, though many had only one. This often meant that children from large families had to sleep three or four to a bed, with two or three beds in a room. Children often slept 'head to toe' in bed.

In some houses where the members of the family worked on a shift system, they also shared the beds on a shift system. Those who worked on night-shifts had the bed during the day, those at work during the day used the same bed at night.

Using the 1881 census, it is possible to work out the number of children in each family. The table shows the results of the 'family size' survey. The totals do *not* include the parents.

Survey of 1881 census results	
Number of Children	Number of Families
0	136
1	128
2	130
3	117
4	87
5	65
6	38
7	27
8	11
9	5
10	1
11	0
12	1
Total number of families 746	

Activities

A

1 Why were Victorian families much larger than families today?
2 Give some of the reasons why the death rate of young children was very high in Victorian times.
3 What do you think was meant by sleeping 'head to toe'?
4 Where in particular did the lack of food and pure water cause many deaths?
5 Many of you will have had chicken pox or measles. Why is it only very rarely that children die from these diseases today?
6 How did some families sleep on a shift system?
7 Farming families were often large. Can you suggest a reason for this?

B

1 Using these results, draw a block graph to show the number of children in each family. Part of the graph has been drawn for you to copy on to graph paper. Complete the graph. (For the vertical axis use 2 cm on the graph paper for every 10 families.)

2 Carry out a 'family size' survey of your class or school. Collect all the results together. Draw a block graph to show your results.

3 Work out the average family size for 1881 and then for your class.

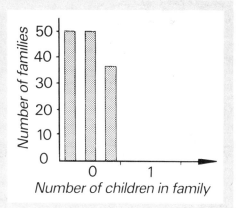

The photograph shows a typical Victorian family. It was taken outside the family cottage in about 1895.
Left to right
(back row): Sam, Jane, Laura, Annie, Jim, Aggie, Bertha, Lizzie, Edward, Mary, George
(centre) Lucy Ann, William (parents)
(front) Ernest, Albert

C Look carefully at the photograph to find the answers to these questions.

1 How many children are there?

2 How many males and how many females are there?

3 Who do you think is the eldest son and the eldest daughter?

4 Describe the clothes worn by Jim, then make a detailed drawing of him.

5 Describe the dress worn by Mary, then make a detailed drawing of her.

6 Sam, Jim, George and William are all wearing something in their waistcoat pockets. What is it?

7 Who is standing two places to the left to Edward?

8 What have Sam, Jim and George got around their necks instead of a tie?

D

1 Try to find out how many children were in the families of:
    (a) your parents
    (b) your grandparents
    (c) your great-grandparents.

2 Make a collection of old family photographs.

3 If you can, find out your family's names and birthdays. You could use this information to build up a simple 'family tree'.

4 Using the 1881 census documents for your own area, discover which is the largest family. How many children are there in the family?

Investigating Occupations

An 'occupation' is a person's job or type of work.

In Burncross in 1881 there were 1185 people who were employed in a total of 140 different jobs. As this was a rural area there were many normal country occupations; there were farmers, a blacksmith and several village shopkeepers.

However, most people in the area were employed either in coal-mining or in the iron and steel industry. Burncross is near Sheffield and at that time Sheffield was the main producer of iron and steel in the country.

There were twenty-seven people who worked on the railways. There had been a single-track railway running through the area since 1854, but in 1876 the track was doubled and the local station was improved, which made more jobs for local people. In the 1871 census for Burncross no one was listed as working on the railways.

Although there were many different jobs, they can be placed into groups of similar types. The table below lists these groups and describes the types of jobs they cover.

Occupation groups	Description of jobs
Mining	People who worked in the coal-mines, underground and on the surface; also mine owners
Iron and steel	People who worked in the making of iron and steel; also some jobs involved in making products from these metals
Farming	People who farmed the land and kept animals (includes farmers, farm workers and servants)
Railways	People who built railways and those who worked on the trains and in the local station
Domestic Service	People who worked as servants looking after the everyday running of the houses and land of wealthy people
Craftsmen	People who were skilled in a special job, usually making things by hand or constructing buildings
Tradesmen	People who sold things, usually from a shop, but sometimes from door to door
Others	People whose jobs do not fit into any of the other occupation groups

Results of occupation survey for Burncross, 1881

Occupation group	Number of people	%	Units for pie chart
Coal-mining	373	32	113°
Iron and steel	276	23	84°
Domestic service	143	12	44°
Farming	68	6	20
Railways	27	2	8°
Craftsmen	188	16	57°
Tradesmen	59	5	18°
Others	51	4	16°
	1185	100	360°

Activities

A

1 Which two occupation groups employed more than 50 per cent of the working population in Burncross in 1881?

2 How many more people worked in coal-mines than on farms?

3 In which groups would these jobs go?
(a) Carpenter   (b) Engine shunter
(c) Stable-boy   (d) Lacemaker
(e) Gamekeeper   (f) Milliner
(g) File-cutter   (h) Ironmonger

4 Draw a pie chart (radius = 6 cm) to show the occupation groups. The units for the chart are in the results table. Use eight different colours. Give your chart a key and a title.

There were some jobs which were common in Victorian times but are no longer carried on today. These jobs have disappeared for many reasons, the most usual being that the skills the people used and the things they made are not in such great demand today. The craftsmen have been replaced by machines which can do the same job much faster and more cheaply. A sawyer is a good example of this. A sawyer was a person who cut up tree trunks and large branches into planks and beams. This was a job for two men with a very large saw. The picture shows the sawyer at work, with a tree trunk placed over a saw-pit; one of the men uses the saw while standing in the pit.

This job is done today by an electric circular saw, which may be controlled by computer. These machines can cut the wood to the exact millimetre required.

Some of the jobs in the list below are still practised today by a few very skilled people.

The Sawyer

B

1 Can you find out what work each of these people would have done? Try to make a drawing of each job.

(a)	Blacksmith	(b)	Wheelwright
(c)	Cordwainer	(d)	Saddler
(e)	Mason	(f)	Toll-bar-keeper
(g)	Wainwright	(h)	Corn miller
(i)	Hawker	(j)	Cabinet-maker

2 Make a list of jobs that were done by hand in the past and are now done by machine.

C   Things to think about

If you have copies of the 1881 census returns for your own area, you could carry out your own investigations.

It would be a good idea to start off by making a tally count of all the different occupations given in your census returns. When you have finished the count, sort out all the occupations into groups. Here are some ideas for you to investigate.

The Cooper

1 What was the main occupation group for your area in 1881?
2 How many farms were in the area in 1881? Are they still there now?
3 Was there a railway station? If so, find out all you can about its history.
4 Were there any shops in 1881? Can you still see them today? Are they still owned by the same families? Make some drawings of the old shops. Have any alterations been made to the buildings?
5 Were there many people involved in domestic service? If so, where? What were their jobs?
6 Do any of the workshops of the craftsmen of the 1880s still exist today?

Investigating
Children at School in 1881

In the 1881 census any child who attended school had to be entered in the 'occupation' column as a 'scholar'. In the Burncross area there were 693 children attending three local schools. These schools catered for an age range of 3½–14 years. The table (below) is divided into two parts: on the left are listed all the children who went to school; on the right are listed all the children who did not go to school.

By the 1880s most children went to school. There was no fixed starting age, so some children did not start school until they were five. This explains the large numbers of three-, four- and five-year-olds who did not go to school. Some parents could not afford to send their children to school especially if it was a large family.

The photograph shows a class of children taken in about 1888. Notice the clothes that the children are wearing. The boys at the front are wearing 'clogs'.

Do you have any old school photographs in your family photograph collection?

Activities

A

1 Draw a block graph to show the numbers of boys and girls of *school age* who went to school in the Burncross area in 1881. Use one-centimetre-squared graph paper. Enter the *ages* on the horizontal axis and the *number of children* on the vertical axis. Use alternate columns for boys and girls, colouring them in different colours.
2 How many children over fourteen attended school?
3 How many children who were of school age did *not* go to school?
4 How many children were at school in the Burncross area in 1881?

B Things to think about

1 Find out about your own school. When was it started and by whom?
2 Look at the census returns for your area. How many children of school age were scholars? How many did not go to school? Can you work out why?

Scholars				At home		
Age	Male	Female	Total	Male	Female	Total
1	1	0	1	28	29	57
2	2	0	2	22	26	48
3	2	1	3	39	23	62
4	20	15	35	48	32	80
5	39	33	72	27	27	54
6	46	37	83	7	7	14
7	29	38	67	9	5	14
8	51	34	85	7	8	15
9	31	31	62	5	9	14
10	36	37	73	8	7	15
11	46	31	77	3	10	13
12	39	29	68	10	6	16
13	23	20	43	6	6	12
14	7	10	17	1	12	13
15	1	3	4	2	11	13
16	0	1	1	1	12	13

School Age (bracketed from age 3 to age 14 in the "At home" section)

Investigating Child Labour Using the 1841 Census

In the 1830s and 1840s children did not have to go to school, mainly because very few day schools existed, and these were usually for the rich.

Many children had to go out to work for a living, to help earn enough money to keep their families in food and clothes. There were no laws controlling the employment of children, which meant that young children were often given tiring and dangerous jobs to do. The employers liked to have children working in their mines, iron and steel works and factories because they did not have to pay them as much as adults.

The information in the chart is taken from the 1841 census for the Burncross area. It lists the jobs of both boys and girls between the ages of eight and fourteen.

The children listed as 'Moulders, Ironworks labourers, Fettlers and Apprentices' would all have worked at the local ironworks. In the 1830s they made a variety of things, including anvils, stoves, flat-irons, pipes, bedsteads, clothes-posts, boot-scrapers and gutters.

Occupation	Ages [in years]							
Boys	8	9	10	11	12	13	14	Totals
Coal-miner	1		3	4	2	2	3	15
Ironstone-miner	1	2	2	1	1	2	1	10
Moulder			2	2	3	2	3	12
Ironworks labourer					2	1		3
Fettler						2	5	7
Apprentice			1	1	3	1		6
Nail-maker			1	1	2	1		5
Male servant					1	1	2	4
Shoemaker							2	2
Screw-maker						1		1
Thread factory worker				1				1
	2	2	9	10	16	11	16	66
Girls								
Female servant		1		1	3		1	6
Ironstone-miner							1	1
		1		1	3		2	7

Activities

A

1 Why did the employers like to use children in the mines?
2 How many children altogether worked in the mines (both coal and ironstone)?
3 What was the age of the youngest female servant?
4 How many children under the age of twelve were employed?
5 What was the age range of the boys who made nails?
6 How many children worked as servants?
7 How old was the girl who worked in the mines?
8 What is 'ironstone'?
9 What do you think would have been made in a 'thread factory'?
10 What was a 'fettler'?
11 If you had to do one of these jobs, which would you choose?

B   Things to think about

1 Find out about other jobs done by children in the 1830s and 1840s, e.g. mill workers, chimney-sweeps.
2 Find out as much as you can about the Earl of Shaftesbury and other factory reformers of the nineteenth century.

Investigating Child Labour in the 1840s

This pie chart shows how a child would have spent a working day in the 1840s.

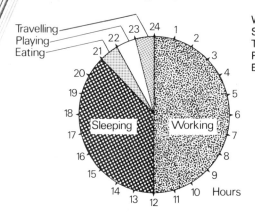

Working	12 hours
Sleeping	9 hours
Travelling	1 hour
Playing	1 hour
Eating	1 hour

In the 1840s working children spent half their day at work. There was no public transport of any kind, so the children had to walk to and from work. The walk home in the evening would have been very tiring after a twelve-hour shift. They might have had time for playing after their evening meal or they might have gone straight to bed, depending on how tired they were.

The children who worked in the mines would have had one of the following jobs to do.

Some of the children were responsible for looking after and leading the ponies used for pulling the waggons underground: they were known as 'drivers'. There were also the 'trappers' who opened and closed the 'traps' (ventilation doors) for the 'corves' (trucks) of coal. These corves could carry 100–500 kilograms of coal.

Activities

1 What is a 'corve'?
2 How many children were drowned in the mines in 1838?
3 How many children under the age of thirteen died in the mines in 1838?
4 Thirteen children were killed by gas explosions. Find out about the 'safety lamp'. Who invented it? How did it work?
5 Read page 19, then imagine that you are a 'trapper' or a 'hurrier'. Describe your working day. Describe your feelings about working underground.
6 Draw a pie chart like the one on this page to show your day. Work out how long you spend doing each of the activities shown.

Children under thirteen

Cause of Death	Number
Fell down the shafts	13
Fell down the shaft due to the rope breaking	1
Fell down when ascending	0
Drawn over the pulley	3
Fall of stone out of a skip down the shaft	1
Drowned in the mines	3
Fall of stones, coal and rubbish in the mines	14
Died from injuries in the mines—not specified	6
Crushed in coal-pits	0
Explosion of gas	13
Suffocated by choke-damp	0
Explosion of gunpowder	0
By tram-wagons	4

1d DAILY NEWS

17th SEPTEMBER 1842
ISSUE: 3452

CHILDREN in the MINES

The recent report tells of many children working underground in terrible conditions. Most of the tunnels are no more than four feet square. Underground springs provide a continual trickle of water, resulting in the floor being 'sloppy and muddy'. Most of the passages are not properly lit and the children have to work in the dark. Some of the younger children come out of the pits so tired after six days work, they sleep the whole of Sunday; some even have to be carried out of the pit.

Daniel Drenchfield
'I am going on ten. I am more tired in the forenoon than at night; it makes my back ache; I work all day ... I rest me when I go home at night; I never go out to play at night; I get my supper and go to bed. Sunday I believe to be the day for recreation; but in the case of some of the girls working in the pits they have occasionally to lie in bed on Sundays to rest themselves for Monday's work.'

WAGES
A trapper usually earns 6d. a day. The hurriers and the other children in the thick-coal pits earn about 5s. a week.

TRAPPERS
John Saville: *seven years old*
'I stand and open and shut the door; I'm generally in the dark, and sit me down against the door; I stop twelve hours in the pit; I never see daylight now except on Sunday. I fell asleep one day, and a corve ran over my leg and made it smart; they'd squeeze me against the door if I fell asleep again.'

Sarah Gooder: *aged eight years*
'I have to trap without a light, and I'm scared. I go at four and sometimes half-past three in the mornings, and come out at five and half-past, I never go to sleep. I sing sometimes when I've light, but not in the dark; I dare not sing then. I don't like being in the pit. I am very sleepy when I go sometimes in the morning.'

CLEANLINESS
'There is no cleaning of anything or anybody either in or near the coal-pits; dirtiness prevails; and no washing is either practised or possible till work is over and the people at home ... even at home washing is partial.'

FOOD AND CLOTHING
'It is a general practice among colliers to breakfast before they go to the pit, and to take their main meal after they return home. The meal taken in the pit is bread, and sometimes bread and meat or bread and cheese. They have oatmeal porridge and milk for breakfast, and sometimes onion porridge. They have meat and potatoes for dinner when they come out of the pit, with milk or ale to drink.'

'The girls employed as hurriers commonly work naked down to the waist, the boys also work naked to the waist, both are dressed in a loose pair of trousers.'

TRAMMERS (or Hurriers)
Patrick Kilbride
'I am eleven years old. I'm a hurrier. I have been in the pit about a year. Before I used to go about begging. I hurry along the maingate about 250 yards. It's level. Another boy hurries with me and I leather him sometimes. I sometimes get leathered myself. I ain't leathered much. I think I sometimes deserve it, but not always. Sometimes my work tires me, but I've never been badly [ill], I like my work middling well. I'd rather be in the pit than beg. They wouldn't keep me if I went to school.'

George Brummitt
'I work in Newton Chambers shallow pit. I am ten years old. I hurry along the level and up the board gates. There is always someone to help me. We go into the pit mostly at five in the morning and come out sometimes before five in the evening. We dine at twelve and stop a quarter of an hour or more sometimes and then go to help fill up a corve [wagon]. I like being there but I'd rather be at school. I don't know how long I have been in the pit. I go to Sunday School every Sunday.'

Investigating
Domestic Service

In the 1880s more than one million people were employed as servants in Britain. Many families had servants to look after them and their houses.

At this time there were many large country houses, owned by wealthy landowners, noblemen and members of the royal family. Some of these houses employed more than 200 servants to work in the house and on the estate. (An 'estate' is the land and other buildings that go with a large house.) In some houses there was a servant to do every single job, including lighting the fires and lamps, greeting visitors and carrying their luggage, cleaning the silver, serving at the table, winding up and cleaning the clocks, cleaning boots and shoes, and many other different jobs.

Servants were used not only by very rich or 'upper-class' families; many 'middle-class' families employed two or three servants, or even more. In Victorian times if a person was able to afford to employ servants it usually meant that he was an important member of the community. Most shopkeepers, innkeepers, business men, managers, doctors and merchants had servants. Often these servants helped to look after the house and the family, as well as helping out in the family business.

Here is an example of a typical family living in Sheffield.

Montague J. Dalton	Head	Mar.	55	Retired Ivory Merchant	Sheffield, Yorkshire
Maud Dalton	Wife	Mar.	39		-do- -do-
Hannah Cooper	Serv.	Unm.	20	Cook	Derbyshire
Mary E. Flowers	Serv.	Unm.	22	Housemaid	Sheffield, Yorkshire

Mr Dalton was a retired merchant. He had two servants to look after himself and his wife. He had a cook to prepare the food and a housemaid to keep the house clean.

Activities

A

1 How many people were employed as servants in Britain in the 1880s?

2 Why did people like to employ servants in Victorian times?

3 What is a 'merchant'?

In 1881 there were 143 people employed as domestic servants in the Burncross area. The list on the right shows the total number of people employed as servants and the different jobs they did.

B Using this information, draw a block graph to show the number of people in service and their different jobs.

Use one-centimetre-squared graph paper. The scale on the vertical axis should be 1cm = 1 person. If any job has more than twenty-five people, then split the number of people into the number of columns needed. Place the jobs in order, from the largest number to the smallest number.

Housemaid	25
Servant	75
Butler	1
Charwoman	3
Groom	5
Governess	3
Errand boy	3
Gardener	10
Housekeeper	8
Coachman	3
Cook	3
Nurse	4
	143

This is **Barnes Hall.** It is a large country house on the outskirts of Burncross. The photograph shows the Hall as it would have looked in the 1880s.

During the 1960s the Hall was converted into three luxury flats which are still occupied today.

The extract from the 1881 census (below) gives details of the owners of the Hall and the servants who worked there. Those marked with an asterisk lived in the Hall. The others lived in cottages near the Hall.

Name	Relation	Condition	Age	Occupation	Birthplace
William Smith	Head	Widr	85	Retired Solicitor	Ecclesfield, Yorkshire
Colin Smith	Son	Unm.	33	Solicitor	Ecclesfield, Yorkshire
Margaret Smith	Dau.	Unm.	47		Ecclesfield, Yorkshire
Maud Smith	Gr. Dau.	(Visitor)	11		London
Florence Smith	Gr. Dau	-do-	9		Dublin
Lucy Webster		Unm.	25	Governess	London
Eliz. Hullyer	*Serv.	-do-	33	Servant	Cambridge
Ann Machen	*Serv.	-do-	27	Servant	Ecclesfield, Yorkshire
Ellen Machen	*Serv.	-do-	21	Servant	-do- -do-
Sarah Jackson	*Serv.	-do-	24	Servant	-do- -do-
Mary Willington	*Serv.	-do-	19	Servant	Stanton, Derbyshire
Thomas Kirkby	Head	Mar.	50	Gardener	Nottingham
Sarah Kirkby	Wife	Mar.	45		Nottingham
Harriet Kirkby	Dau.	Unm.	16	Maid	Ecclesfield, Yorkshire
Joseph Kirkby	Son	Unm.	14	Gardener	-do- -do-
William Smith	Head	Mar.	34	Butler	Folkingham, Lincolnshire
Elizabeth Smith	Wife	Mar.	34		Tickhill, Yorkshire
Lucy Smith	Dau.	Unm.	11	Scholar	Ecclesfield, Yorkshire
John Gray	Lodger	Unm.	20	Groom	Hoyland, Yorkshire
William Taylor	Head	Mar.	40	Coachman	Leicestershire
Agnes Taylor	Wife	Mar.	32		Sevenoaks, Kent
Charles Carter	Lodger	Unm.	23	Groom/Domestic	Benwich, Cambridgeshire

C

1 Who was the head of the household?
2 How many servants worked at Barnes Hall?
3 What was the occupation of Colin Smith?
4 How many servants actually lived in the Hall?
5 Where was the Butler born?
6 What was the name of the lodger who lived with the Smith family?
7 How many visitors were at the Hall?
8 Why do you think that a coachman and two grooms were employed at the Hall?
9 What is a 'governess'?
10 What relation to each other are the two gardeners?
11 How many servants were born outside the parish of Ecclesfield?
12 Why do you think the Hall was converted into flats in the 1960s?

D Investigate your local manor-house or hall using the 1881 census. Try to find out about the history of the building and the people who lived and worked there. Make a collection of photographs and drawings.

Investigating Housing 1

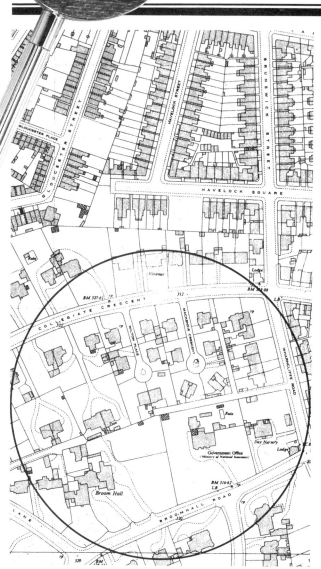

It is interesting to compare two areas or streets within the same town. The Ordnance Survey map and the 1881 census documents together can give a clear picture of life in any area. The next four pages show how you can investigate differences in housing in your own area.

The Enumerators' Returns should give the name of the street or road and also the number of the house where each person lived. Using this information, it is possible to locate some of the houses recorded in the census.

In the 1880s this area of Sheffield provided two very different types of housing. Within a few hundred yards of each other there were large Victorian mansions and small back-to-back houses. These can be clearly seen on the map.

In Victorian Sheffield the area shown in the circle contained large houses lived in by wealthy people.

The photograph shows the lodge at the end of Broomhall Road. In the 1880s there would have been a gate across the road. This was to stop anyone, other than the residents and their visitors, using the road. The lodge can be found on the map and in the census extract on the next page.

In the 1880s only wealthy people could afford to buy houses in this area. The people who lived here owned factories or steelworks or had some form of business. There were also business people who had made their fortunes and then retired here.

As you can see from the map, the gardens and grounds of these houses are very large. Most of the owners employed several servants to look after their houses for them.

The following examples are taken from the 1881 census.

7 Collegiate Cres.	John Jackson	Head	Mar.	58	Chief Constable
	Sarah M. Jackson	Wife	Mar.	53	
	Mary Lazenby	Serv.	Unm.	27	General Servant
	Helen Hirst	Serv.	Unm.	17	General Servant
3 Wilton Place	Wm Rutherford	Head	Unm.	79	Retired Metal Agent
	Elizabeth -do-	Niece	Unm.	48	
	Mary Bartlett		Unm.	26	Lady's Companion
	Emma Roe	Serv.	Unm.	28	General Servant
9 Collegiate Cres.	Wm Wilson	Head	Mar.	45	Coach Builder (30 men)
	Harriet Wilson	Wife	Mar.	45	
	Gertrude Wilson	Daut.	Unm.	19	
	Eliza Potts	Serv.	Unm.	26	General Servant
	Bertha Nicholls	Serv.	Unm.	19	General Servant
1 The Elms	Wm L. Austin	Head	Mar.	56	Steel & File Manufacturer
	Mary Austin	Wife	Mar.	58	(79 men, 13 boys, 6 women)
	Ann Austin	Daut.	Unm.	30	
	George Austin	Son	Unm.	26	Merchant's Apprentice
	Marta Shadall	Serv.	Unm.	21	General Servant
Lodge 2 Broomhall Rd	Thomas Bowler	Head	Mar.	36	Gardener
	Emma Bowler	Wife	Mar.	36	
	Emma Hudson	Lodger	Unm.	24	Engraver's Assistant
	Elizabeth Williams	Visitor		24	(Blind)
	Emily Bradley	-do-		11	Guide to Blind Lady

Activities

A

1 What job did John Jackson have? Was this an important job?
2 How many servants did he employ? What were their names?
3 What name do you think 'Wm' is short for? How many people had this name in these examples?
4 What job did Mary Bartlett have? What do you think this meant?
5 Who owned a coach-building business?

B Things to think about

1 Using the map, estimate how many times larger are the houses in Collegiate Crescent than those in Gloucester Street.
2 The photograph at the top of page 22 shows a house in Collegiate Crescent. Why did the owners have servants?
3 Most people do not have servants nowadays. Why have many of the houses in Collegiate Crescent been divided into flats?

All the houses shown within the circle can still be seen today. Most of them are still lived in, some by one family while others have been converted into flats. Some of the mansions which are too large and too expensive for modern family houses have been taken over by the City Polytechnic. One of these is shown in the photograph.

Investigating
Housing 2

The area in the circle contained rows of terraced houses. Many of these were back-to-back. In the 1880s this area was lived in by the working people of Sheffield.

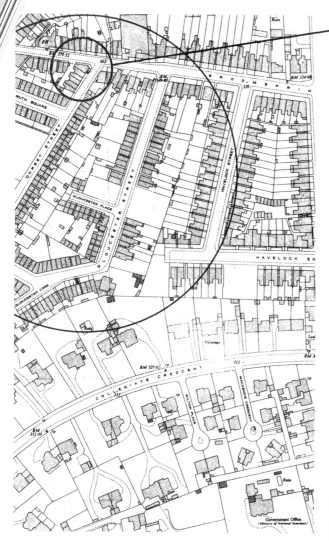

Some of the streets contained houses with doors opening straight on to the road.

Some of the people who lived in this area were craftsmen. Many others worked in the factories and the steelworks owned by the people who lived in the mansions nearby.

Back-to-back terraced houses

1a	1b
2a	2b

The back-to-back houses in this area were built in groups of four. The toilets for all four houses were in the backyard.

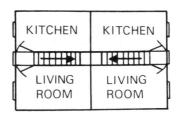

DOWNSTAIRS

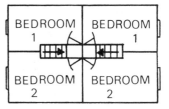

UPSTAIRS

These plans show the upstairs and downstairs of two back-to-back houses.

These examples from the 1881 census are within the area marked on the map.

34 Gloucester St.	Wilfred Biggin	Head	Mar.	31	Silversmith (handle maker)
	Belinda Biggin	Wife	Mar.	28	
29 Gloucester St.	Sarah A. Kay	Head	Widow	57	Retired Grocer
	Benjamin Kay	Son	Unm.	31	Cooper
7 Dorset Street	Joseph Higgins	Head	Mar.	49	Police Sergeant
	Ann Higgins	Wife	Mar.	50	
	Samuel Higgins	Son	Unm.	24	Cabinet Maker
	Ann Cherry	Daut.	Mar.	22	Dressmaker
	Chas. H. Cherry	Son-in-law	Mar.	22	Joiner
51 Dorset Street	Maria Wyatt	Head	Widow	53	
	George A. Wyatt	Son	Unm.	21	Cab Driver
	Elizabeth Wyatt	Daut.	Unm.	23	Sewing Machinist
53 Dorset Street	Arthur Booth	Head	Mar.	31	Scissor Smith
	Eliza Booth	Wife	Mar.	30	
	William H. Booth	Son	Unm.	8	Scholar
	Clement Booth	Son		6	Scholar
	Lillie Booth	Daut.		4	
	Eliza Booth	Daut.		2	
	Arthur Booth	Son		3 weeks	
Ct. 17 No: 1 Dorset Street	Allen Eastwood	Head	Mar.	37	Table Knife Forger
	Ann Eastwood	Wife	Mar.	34	
Ct. 17 No: 2 Dorset Street	William Hodgekinson	Head	Mar.	58	Coachman/Servant
	Sarah A. Hodgekinson	Wife	Mar.	52	
	Mary Hodgekinson	Daut.	Unm.	22	School Mistress (Assistant)
	Samuel Hodgekinson	Son		15	Clerk (Solicitor General)

These houses formed a block of four back-to-back houses

All the back-to-back houses in this area have now been demolished. The area has been redeveloped to form a modern housing estate, with some detached houses and some old people's bungalows. Grass and trees have been planted to give a 'landscaped' appearance.

Activities

A

1 How many people were employed in the knife or scissor industries?
2 What was Sarah Kay's job before she retired?
3 Her son was a cooper. What was that?
4 How many people lived in this block of back-to-back houses?
5 George Wyatt was a cab driver. What type of cab would this have been?
6 How many rooms were there in a back-to-back house?
7 Find Dorset Street on the map and count the number of back-to-back houses in the street.
8 Did these houses have any gardens?

B Things to think about

1 Why do you think that the people in the Dorset Street area had no servants?
2 The back-to-back houses were demolished because they were regarded as 'slums'. Why were they not good places to live in?

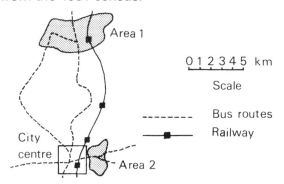

Investigating
Travelling to Work
Using the 1981 Census

The results of the 1981 census provide a vast amount of information about the everyday life of people in the 1980s.

This investigation is based on the results of a census survey on how people travel to work, which was one of the questions in the 1981 census. These results are taken from the 'Small Area Statistics' for two different areas of a large city.

The map below shows the position of these two areas in relation to the city centre. The table gives some of the population and housing results for each area, taken from the 1981 census.

Scale: 0 1 2 3 4 5 km

-------- Bus routes

━■━ Railway

	Area 1: suburb	Area 2: inner city
Distance from the city centre	11 km	1½ km
Population 1971	16 825	18 525
Population 1981	22 647	17 754
Area in hectares	1060 ha.	336 ha.
Persons per hectare	21.3	52.8
Total number of households	7 895	7 403
Private housing	60.9%	8.7%
Rented from council	34.8%	87.9%
Households with a car	64.1%	29.6%
Population under 16 years	25.8%	17.8%
Population over pensionable age	12.8%	25.0%

Activities

A Use the information in the map and the table to answer these questions.

1 Which area is nearer to the city centre?

2 Which area had a large increase in population between 1971 and 1981? By how many people did it increase?

3 By how many has the population fallen in the other area?

If we divide the population by the number of hectares in each area we find the 'population density'. In other words, it tells us *how many people there are for each hectare of land.*

4 Which area has the higher population density?

5 How many more people per hectare are there in the inner city than in the suburb?

As you have just seen, the area of the inner city is very small compared with the suburb, yet there are more than twice as many people per hectare in the inner city than the suburb.

6 The houses in the suburb are mainly detached and semi-detached. Which of the following do you think are the main types of housing in the inner-city area?
Terraced   Detached   Semi-detached   High-rise flats   Maisonettes

7 Which area has the larger amount of private housing?

8 Which area has more council housing?

9 Which area has the higher number of households with a car?

10 In which area do you think new houses are still being built?

The table below shows the results of the 'travelling to work' survey for the two areas already described. The information is taken from the 1981 census.

This type of survey is known as a '10 per cent sample'. This means that only one-tenth of the census return forms were used in the survey, instead of all the forms. Therefore, this is a survey of *one person in every ten* who live in the area.

10% sample	Methods of Transport												Type of Work		
	CAR [pool/sharing]	CAR [passenger]	CAR [driver]	BUS	B.R. TRAIN	UNDERGROUND	MOTOR CYCLE	PEDAL CYCLE	ON FOOT	OTHERS	WORK AT HOME		FULL TIME	PART TIME	WORK OUTSIDE DISTRICT
Suburb area	26	79	356	259	12	0	24	6	119	11	14		773	191	127
Inner city area	23	26	147	420	4	0	14	1	73	8	7		558	170	41

'Car (pool/sharing)' means that a group of car owners take it in turns to use their cars to give the others a lift to work.

There is no underground transport system in the city.

B
1 How many people altogether (full-time and part-time) work in: (i) the suburb? (ii) the inner-city area?
2 Which area has more people working outside the district?
3 In which area do more people use buses than cars for travelling to work?
4 What do you think 'work at home' means?
5 Which area has the higher number of people who walk to work?
6 Which two methods of travel are used by a total of thirty people in the suburb?
7 How many more people use cars than buses in the suburb?
8 There are high numbers of part-time workers in both areas: are most of these likely to be male or female workers? Explain why.

C Draw a block graph for each area to show the methods of transport used for travelling to work. Use one-centimetre-squared graph paper. On the vertical axis use a scale of 1 cm for ten people. If any column has more people than the maximum extent of the vertical axis, split the total up over a number of columns. Check that your graphs have a title and that the same colours are used for the same columns in each graph.

D Public transport services: buses

This table gives details of the bus services from each area into the city centre on weekdays.

	Area 1: suburb	Area 2: inner city
Number of bus routes into the city centre	11	9
Time interval between buses	15 min.	5 min.
Cost of a single journey into the city centre	60p Adult 30p Child	25p Adult 12p Child
Time taken by bus	30 min.	8 min.
Time taken by car	12 min.	3–4 min.

1 Which area has the more frequent bus service?
2 How long does the journey take by bus from the suburb? Is it quicker by car?
3 If someone from each area travels to and from work in the city centre, how much does it cost each person per week?
4 If it costs 10p per kilometre to travel by car, is it cheaper by car or by bus?

Pupils' Resource Sheets

The numbers shown on Map 1 indicate the county, *not* the number of people born there.

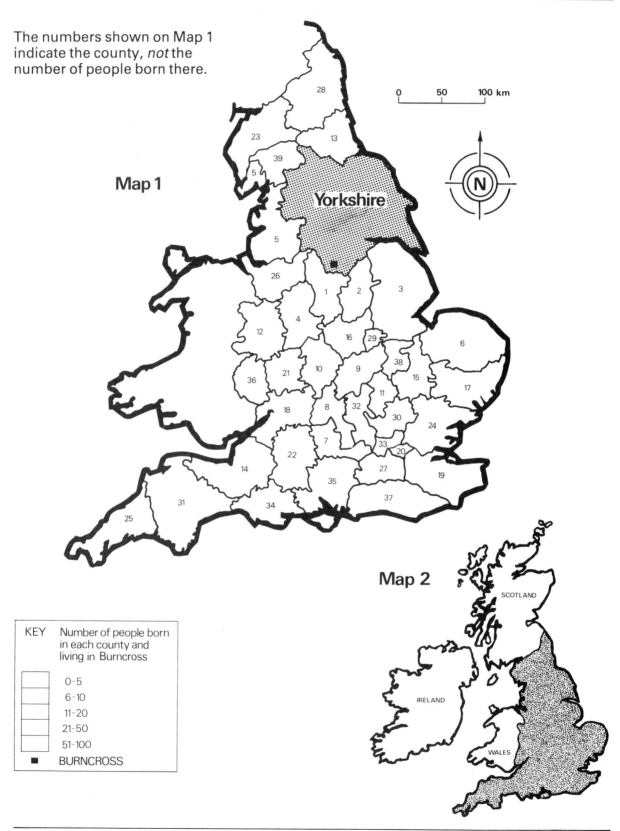

Map 1

Yorkshire

0   50   100 km

N

Map 2

SCOTLAND

IRELAND

WALES

KEY   Number of people born in each county and living in Burncross

0-5

6-10

11-20

21-50

51-100

■   BURNCROSS

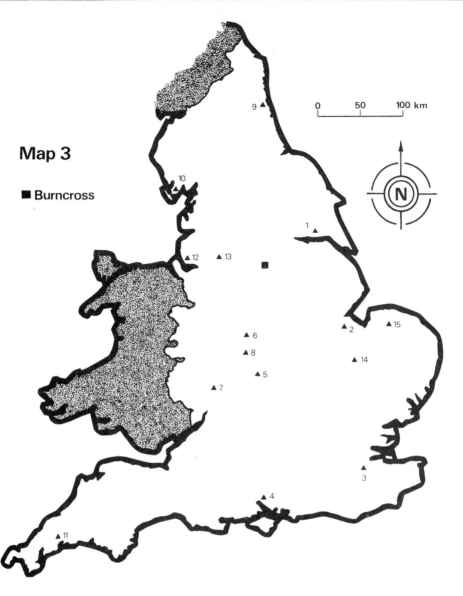

Map 3

■ Burncross

0   50   100 km

N

Number on map	Name	Age	Occupation	Birthplace	Distance from Burncross
1	Sarah Shaw	20	Servant	HULL, Yorkshire	85 km
2					
3					
4					
5					
6					
7					
8					
9					
10					
11					
12					
13					
14					
15					

Notes for Teachers

CONCEPTS
Similarity and difference between the 1880s and the present day:
- general 'life style'.
- occupations and working conditions of both adults and children.
- methods of transport available.
- family size and structure.

Communication:
- movement and migration of people.
- birthplaces other than the local area.

Continuity and change:
- increasing or decreasing population of the local area.
- growth or decline of local industries, resulting in changes in occupations.
- changes in the social structure of the population.

Cause and consequence:
- the 'age of machines' and its effect on industry and occupations.
- availability of jobs resulting in migration to new areas.

AIMS
The aim of this book is to enable the children:
- to be aware of the types of information that are available on census material and how this information may be extracted.
- to be aware of the problems or difficulties which may arise in reading or surveying the census materials.
- to investigate a specific location and to identify and relate to the people who lived there in the 1880s.
- to make a comparison between family sizes of the 1880s and those of today.
- to be aware of the changes in employment and working conditions of adults and children.
- to understand how the needs of Victorian society, and particularly village communities, created jobs in the local area, e.g. blacksmiths, craftsmen and domestic servants.
- to identify different types of occupation, past and present, and to classify these into groups of similar types.
- to investigate the social standards and housing conditions of a Victorian settlement, and to compare the same settlement today.

GENERAL SKILLS
The book helps children to develop skills in:
- extraction of relevant information from original documents.
- using other reference books and materials to supplement and explain the information gathered from the census.
- representing this information in a variety of forms: graphical, factual and creative written and drawing work.
- interpreting statistics in table form.
- using and interpreting maps and photographs.
- the ability to work individually or in groups.
- 'empathizing', i.e. having a creative understanding of the feelings of someone else in another time and another place.
- classifying information.
- evaluating evidence and discovering its reliability.
- using correct vocabulary in its correct context.
- using various drawing apparatus in the construction of graphs and pie charts.
- mapwork: the use of an atlas, a key and a scale.

SPECIFIC SKILLS
The children will need to:
- know how to construct a block graph.
- be familiar with vertical and horizontal axes.
- know how to make a tally count, in lots of five, i.e. 卌
- know how to work out an average number.
- know how to construct a pie chart.
- know how to use a compass and a protractor.
- have a basic understanding of percentages.
- be familiar with a map scale and a key.

MATERIALS
The children will need to have access to the following:
A4-size one-centimetre-squared graph paper

Writing paper	Pencil crayons
Tracing paper	Felt-tip pens
Pair of compasses	Map pins
Protractor	Cotton
Metric ruler	

Copies of a local newspaper
A large-scale map of the local area, either Ordnance Survey or street plan
An atlas
A set of class lists for your school

SOURCES OF CENSUS MATERIALS
The Enumerators' Returns for the censuses from 1841 to 1881 are available at your nearest city/town/county library, where photocopying facilities are usually available.

These Returns are also stored on microfilm, copies of which, for *England and Wales, the Isle of Man, and the Channel Islands only,* may be seen at the Public Record Office in the Land Registry Building, London WC2.

Further details of where to obtain census information, and copies of information sheets about the 1981 census, are available from: Office of Population Censuses and Surveys, St Catherine's House, 10 Kingsway, London WC2B 6JP.

Suggestions for follow-up work

It is important to stress that the activities set out in this book can be used with any census material for any part of the country. The ideas based on the study area of Burncross, can easily be adapted to take account of the features of another area. It is worthwhile making a collection of photocopies of the original Enumerators' Returns for your area: this can be done quite cheaply at the library. If you can afford to copy the documents for one or more Enumeration Districts from the 1881 census, then you will have a useful study area of your own.

What is a census?   pages 4 and 5
The Office of Population Censuses and Surveys has some very useful information sheets that give details of how the 1981 census was organized. These include a comprehensive history of the censuses in Great Britain.

Original 1881 census documents   page 6 and 7
This would be a good time to let the children have a look at some of the census documents for your area.

Forenames   pages 8 and 9
A similar investigation could be made into surnames; there are many reference books available on the origin of names. The children could investigate the origin of their own names. The survey could be taken further by researching the origin of place-names.

Birthplaces   pages 10 and 11
As this investigation shows, there was quite a lot of movement around the country in search of work in the 1880s. Methods of transport were limited in those days. An investigation could be made into the transport of the nineteenth century. The development of the railways would make a good subject for study.

Family size   pages 12 and 13
Some children might be able to develop the idea of a family tree, using information about their own families. A good example of a family tree is that of the royal family. In addition, a class collection of old family photographs could be made.

Occupations   pages 14 and 15
A useful follow-up topic would be to use the 1881 census of your own area to investigate occupations.

It may be possible to make a survey of present-day occupations by finding out the jobs of the children's parents. The results can then be compared with the 1881 survey to find out whether the main occupation groups in your area have changed over the years.

Another subject for investigation could be a comparison of mothers going out to work today with the numbers of mothers going out to work in 1881.

Children at school in 1881   page 16
If yours is an old school there may be some early documents relating to it. There may also be copies of old school record books: these can give a fascinating insight into the history of a school. Additionally, a collection of old school photographs could be made.

Try to find out about the beginning of education in your area.

Child labour in the 1840s   pages 17, 18 and 19
Coal-mines were not the only place where children worked; investigate some of the others. There are many other reports similar to the 1842 Commission on Children in the Mines, copies of which may be available in your library.

A survey could be carried out to find out how many children have regular jobs, such as newspaper rounds or Saturday shop work.

Domestic service   pages 20 and 21
An investigation into your local manor-house or hall could be made, using the 1881 census or even some of the earlier ones. If you know of someone who was in service when they were young, try to record an interview with them for the children to use.

Housing   pages 22, 23, 24 and 25
It may be possible to use the early census material to investigate a specific area as part of a wider environmental topic or theme. You could choose a street or road or a specific building that can be located in the 1881 census, then find out as much as possible about the history and development of that location. This could be developed into a larger theme bringing in scientific and geographical aspects.

It should be noted that it is not always possible to find addresses in the Enumerators' Returns; some of them wrote down only the area and not the name of the road or street.

Another line of investigation might be into the social conditions that existed in the towns and cities in Victorian times.

Methods of travelling to work using the 1981 census   pages 26 and 27
This activity is based on information taken from the 'Small Area Statistics' from the 1981 census. The whole country is divided into very small areas and the results of the 1981 census are available in statistical form for each area: these are called 'Small Area Statistics'. For further information on these write to: Census Customer Services, O.P.C.S., Titchfield, Fareham, Hants. PO15 5RR.

If you use these 'Small Area Statistics' with children in the primary school you may find it advisable first to prepare the statistics into a suitable form for the children to use. As they stand, the documents are one mass of statistics.

Resource sheets   pages 28 and 29
These pages contain specially prepared maps for use with the activities in the investigation into birthplaces on pages 10 and 11.

Consultation with many teachers and advisers has revealed the need for a series which helps to structure topic work in the local environment. Structured investigations into the child's own environment can be a rich source of ideas and motivation leading to work in other disciplines. Each book in the series has the following aims:

- to provide sufficient information and structure **for pupils, either individually or in groups**, to carry out their own investigations into their environment;

- to provide **for those pupils who are unable to go outside the class-room,** sufficient information for them to be able to experience the key ideas concerning the local environment;

- to provide **for the teacher** a set of structured ideas for investigating the environment.

This expanding series has three areas of concern, each with a number of titles.

PEOPLE AND MOVEMENT
Investigating Recreation
Investigating Census Materials
Investigating Traffic
Investigating Streets, Bridges and Tunnels

THE NATURAL ENVIRONMENT
Investigating Weather
Investigating Pollution and Conservation
Investigating Rivers and Ponds
Investigating Woods, Hedges and Grassland

TOWN AND VILLAGE
Investigating Homes
Investigating Town and Village Patterns
Investigating Schools
Investigating Places of Worship

Details of all these and other titles can be found in the Arnold-Wheaton catalogue.